BOOK 3 - Drums & Mallet Percussion

STANDARD OF EXCELLENCE

COMPREHENSIVE BAND METHOD

By Bruce Pearson

Dear Student:

Welcome to STANDARD OF EXCELLENCE Book 3.

By now, you have demonstrated that you are making steady progress toward becoming an accomplished musician. With the skills you are mastering, you are beginning to realize the value of hard work and the joy of music-making.

STANDARD OF EXCELLENCE Book 3 introduces you to some of the world's finest music. By performing this literature, you will gain an appreciation for a variety of musical styles while improving your individual instrument and ensemble skills.

Best wishes as you explore Book 3.

Sincerely,

Bruce Pearson

Practicing - the key to EXCELLENCE!

▶ Make practicing part of your daily schedule. If you plan it as you do any other activity, you will find plenty of time for it.
▶ Try to practice in the same place every day. Choose a place where you can concentrate on making music. Start with a regular and familiar warm-up routine, including Rudiments and simple technical exercises. Like an athlete, you need to warm-up your mind and muscles before you begin performing.
▶ Set goals for every practice session. Keep track of your practice time and progress on the front cover Practice Journal.
▶ Practice the hard spots in your lesson assignments and band music over and over, until you can play them perfectly.
▶ Make time for practice on drums, mallet percussion instruments, and any other percussion instruments you are studying individually or playing in band.
▶ At the end of each practice session, play something fun.

Also Available: STANDARD OF EXCELLENCE Timpani & Auxiliary Percussion Book 3 (W23TM).

SPECIAL NOTE: Pages 38-40 are not included for drums in this book. Play mallet percussion instruments or timpani when the band is playing from these pages.

ISBN 0-8497-5991-9

kjos NEIL A. KJOS MUSIC COMPANY, PUBLISHER

W23PR

REVIEW

NINE STROKE ROLL

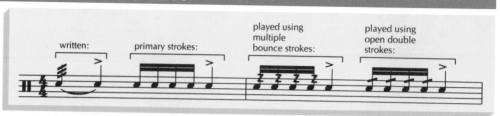

FIVE STROKE ROLL

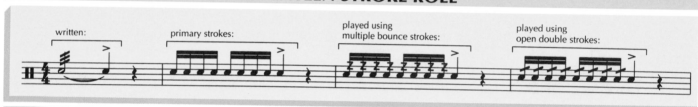

SEVENTEEN STROKE ROLL

1 WARM-UP - Band Arrangement
Page 44 ▐▐▐▶

Andante

▶ This exercise may also be played on drum set.

▶ When you see a page number followed by an arrow, *Excellerate* to the page indicated for additional studies.

2 TECHNIQUE BREAK

Moderato

▶ Practice the rolls two ways: 1. Using multiple bounce strokes; 2. Using open double strokes.

3 RIG A JIG JIG

American Folk Song

Moderato

4 - Tacet ▶ See "Mallets" page 2.

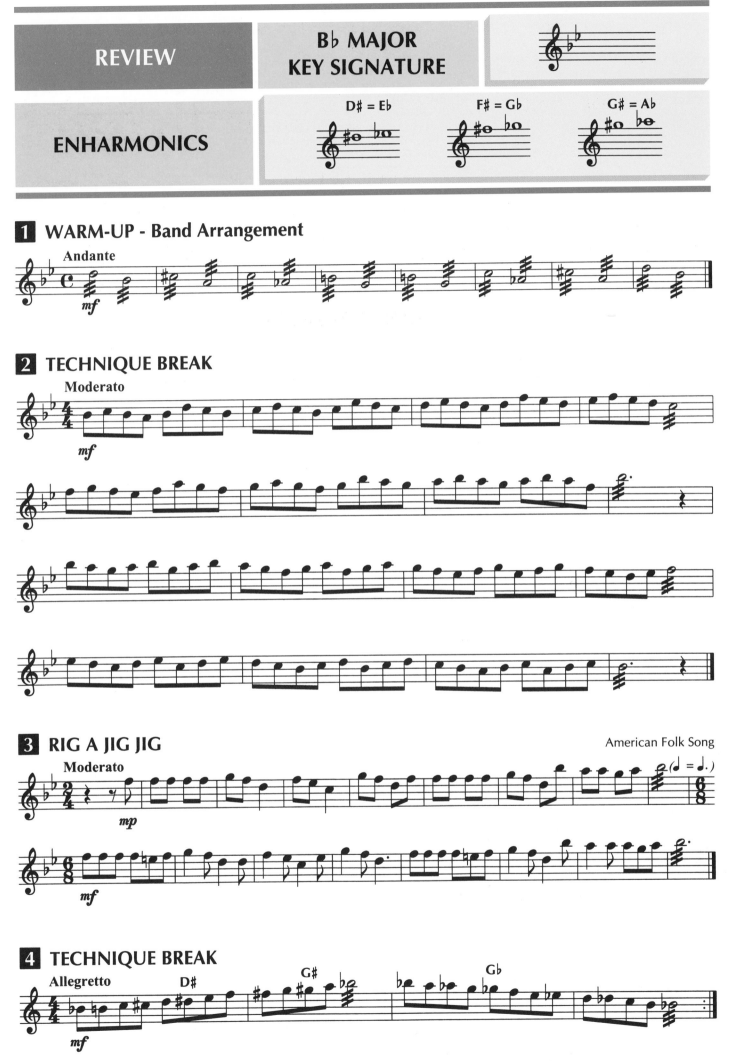

REVIEW

ROLLS IN ¢

NINE STROKE ROLL

FIVE STROKE ROLL

SEVENTEEN STROKE ROLL

5 G MINOR SCALE SKILL

Moderato

Natural Minor

Harmonic Minor

Melodic Minor · Arpeggio · Chords

6 PAT-A-PAN

French Carol

Moderato

snares off

7 / 8 - Tacet ▶ See "Mallets" page 3.

9 GO FOR EXCELLENCE!

Allegro

▶ Lines with a medal are *Achievement Lines.* The chart on the last page of the book can be used to record your progress.

| **REVIEW** | **G MINOR KEY SIGNATURE** | 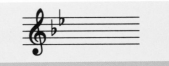 |

5 G MINOR SCALE SKILL

6 PAT-A-PAN

French Carol

7 INTERVAL INQUISITION

▶ Write in the intervals on the lines provided.

8 ARTICULATION ADVENTURE

9 GO FOR EXCELLENCE!

▶ Lines with a medal are *Achievement Lines.* The chart on the inside back cover can be used to record your progress.

 **REVIEW** **SEVEN STROKE ROLL**

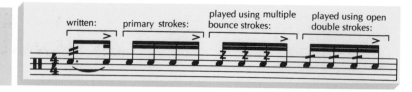

written: | primary strokes: | played using multiple bounce strokes: | played using open double strokes:

DYNAMICS

fortissimo (**ff**) - very loud   *pianissimo* (**pp**) - very soft

SIXTEENTH NOTES IN
3/8 & 6/8 TIME

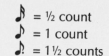

A single sixteenth note is half as long as an eighth note.

PLAYING A BASS DRUM ROLL

Hold a large-headed medium-soft bass drum beater in each hand. Be sure two beaters of the same size, style, and weight are used. Create the roll by playing alternating single strokes on the head. Strike the head in the area between the center of the head and the rim. Use slow to moderately slow strokes to create the roll.

10 DYNAMIC DYNAMICS

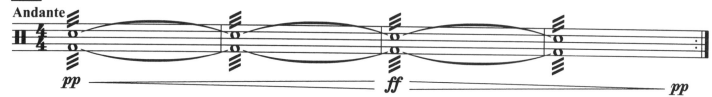

11 - Tacet ▶ See "Mallets" page 4.

12 TECHNIQUE BREAK

▶ Be sure that all your strokes sound the same.

13 MY PARTNER AND I

Swedish Folk Dance

14 FOR SNARE DRUMS ONLY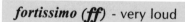

▶ Write in the counting and clap the rhythm before you play.

REVIEW	Eb MAJOR KEY SIGNATURE	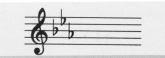

MAJOR CHORD		MINOR CHORD	

DYNAMICS	*fortissimo* (**ff**) - very loud *pianissimo* (**pp**) - very soft

10 DYNAMIC DYNAMICS

Andante

11 MAJOR AND MINOR CHORD EAR TRAINER

Page 44

Major Chord   Minor Chord

1 3 1 5 1 3 5 3 1   1 3 1 5 1 3 5 3 1

▶ Sing before you play.

12 TECHNIQUE BREAK

Moderato

13 MY PARTNER AND I

Swedish Folk Dance

Allegretto

14 FOR MALLETS ONLY

Moderato

STYLE | *simile* - Continue playing in the same manner.

15 CHORALE - Band Arrangement

John B. Dykes (1823 - 1876)

16 C MINOR SCALE SKILL

17 TUMBALALAIKA

Jewish Folk Song

18 TECHNIQUE BREAK

19 GO FOR EXCELLENCE!

REVIEW

C MINOR KEY SIGNATURE

ENHARMONICS

A# = Bb

15 CHORALE - Band Arrangement

John B. Dykes (1823 - 1876)

Largo

mp legato

mf *mp*

16 C MINOR SCALE SKILL

Moderato

Natural Minor

Harmonic Minor

mf

Melodic Minor

Arpeggio

Chords

17 TUMBALALAIKA

Jewish Folk Song

Moderato

mf

1. 2.

18 TECHNIQUE BREAK

Allegretto

mp

1. 2.

19 GO FOR EXCELLENCE!

Andante

A#

mf *ff* *pp*

ROLLS IN $\frac{3}{8}$ & $\frac{6}{8}$

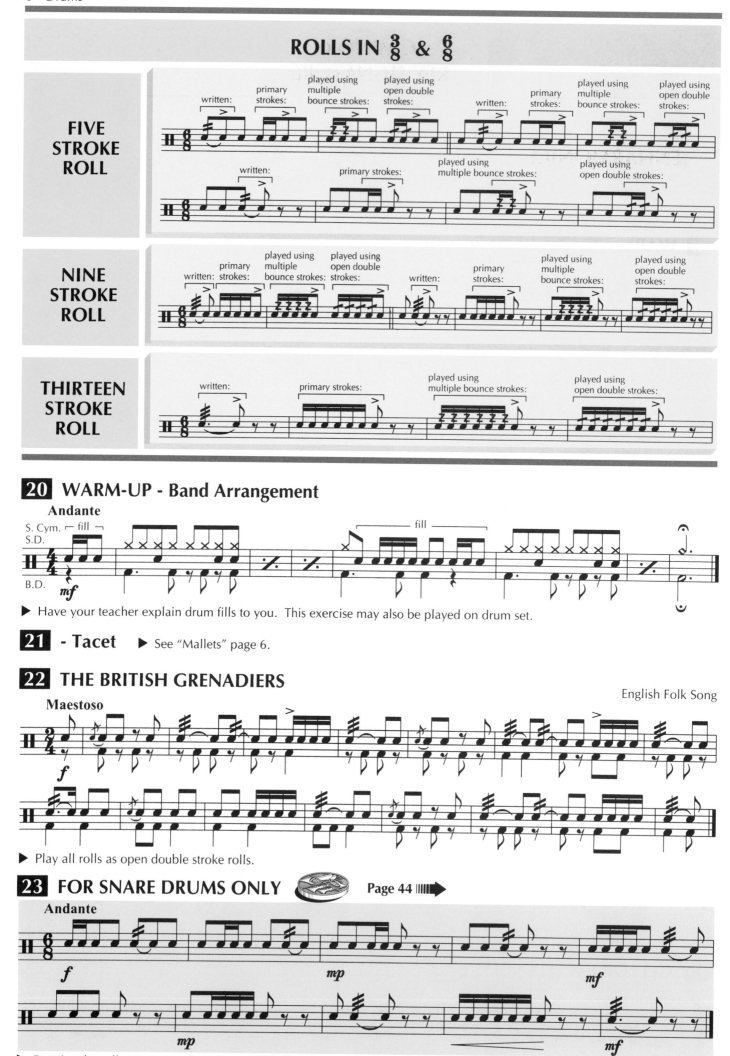

FIVE STROKE ROLL

NINE STROKE ROLL

THIRTEEN STROKE ROLL

20 WARM-UP - Band Arrangement

Andante

▶ Have your teacher explain drum fills to you. This exercise may also be played on drum set.

21 - Tacet   ▶ See "Mallets" page 6.

22 THE BRITISH GRENADIERS

English Folk Song

Maestoso

▶ Play all rolls as open double stroke rolls.

23 FOR SNARE DRUMS ONLY   Page 44 ▶

Andante

▶ Practice the rolls two ways: 1. Using multiple bounce strokes; 2. Using open double strokes.

| REVIEW | F MAJOR KEY SIGNATURE | |
| ENHARMONICS | | |

G# = Ab   A# = Bb

20 WARM-UP - Band Arrangement

Andante

21 TECHNIQUE BREAK

Moderato

22 THE BRITISH GRENADIERS

English Folk Song

Maestoso

23 FOR MALLETS ONLY

Andante

G#   A#

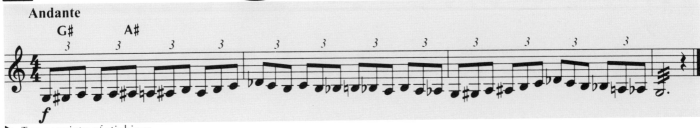

▶ Try a variety of stickings.

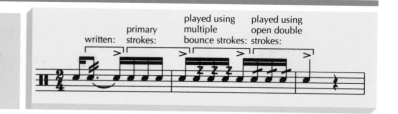

REVIEW | **SEVEN STROKE ROLL**

24 C MAJOR SCALE SKILL

25 ARTICULATION ADVENTURE

▶ Write in the counting before you play.

26 GREEN GROW THE RASHES O

Scottish Folk Song

27 TECHNIQUE BREAK

28 GO FOR EXCELLENCE!

Scottish Folk Song

"Bonnie Glen Shee"

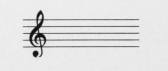

REVIEW

C MAJOR KEY SIGNATURE

SIXTEENTH/ DOTTED EIGHTH NOTE COMBINATION

24 C MAJOR SCALE SKILL

Arpeggio   Chords

25 ARTICULATION ADVENTURE

▶ Write in the counting for the top line before you play.

26 GREEN GROW THE RASHES O

Scottish Folk Song

27 TECHNIQUE BREAK

28 GO FOR EXCELLENCE!

Scottish Folk Song

"Bonnie Glen Shee"

SIXTEENTH/EIGHTH/ SIXTEENTH NOTE COMBINATION

TRIPLE PARADIDDLE

R L R L R L R R L R L R L R L L

The triple paradiddle is a Rudiment.

29 A♭ MAJOR SCALE SKILL

Moderato

Arpeggio   Chords

30 ARTICULATION ADVENTURE

Allegretto

▶ Write in the counting before you play.

31 LA RASPA

Mexican Folk Song

Allegretto

mp - 1st time

f - 2nd time

32 TECHNIQUE BREAK

Andante
Triple Paradiddle

R L R L R L R L R R L   L R   R L   L R   L R L R L R L R L L R   R L   L R   R L

> *simile*   R L   L R L   L R   R L   L R   R L

mf

ff   *mf*

R L R L R L R L R R L   L R   R L   L R   L R L R L R L R L L R   R L   L R   R L   R L   L R L   L R   L L

mp

▶ On accented rolls, accent the first stroke only.

REVIEW

Ab MAJOR KEY SIGNATURE

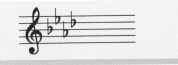

SIXTEENTH/EIGHTH/ SIXTEENTH NOTE COMBINATION

ENHARMONICS

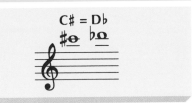

C# = Db

29 Ab MAJOR SCALE SKILL

Moderato Arpeggio Chords

f

30 ARTICULATION ADVENTURE

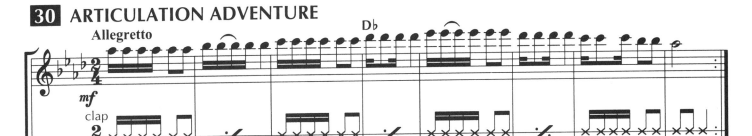

Allegretto Db

mf

clap

▶ Write in the counting for the top line before you play.

31 LA RASPA

Mexican Folk Song

Allegretto

mp - 1st time
f - 2nd time

32 TECHNIQUE BREAK

Andante

mf

ff *mf*

mp

33 **- Tacet** ▶ See "Mallets" page 9.

34 **TECHNIQUE BREAK** Page 44 ◼◼◼▶

Andante

35 _____ Composer _____

your name

▶ Compose a duet for snare drum and bass drum.

36 **- Tacet** ▶ See "Mallets" page 9.

37 **GO FOR EXCELLENCE!**

Korean Folk Song

Andante
"Arirang"

S. Cym. with S.D. stick
S.D. rim
S.D. head with snares off
B.D. with S.D. stick

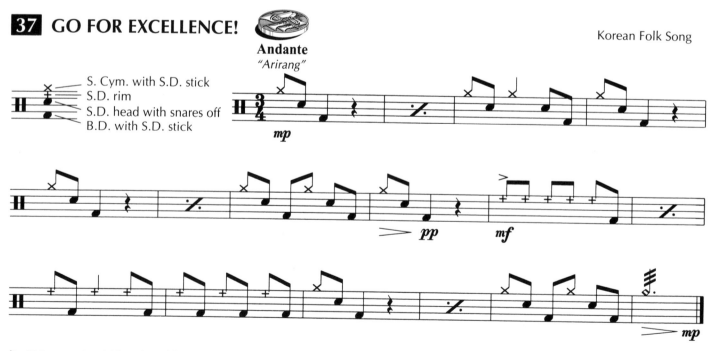

▶ This part should be played by one percussionist. Play the S. Cym. roll using single strokes.
▶ When playing this exercise, let the S. Cym. and B.D. ring freely after striking.

33 LONDONDERRY AIR - Band Arrangement

Irish Folk Song
arr. Bruce Pearson (b. 1942)

34 TECHNIQUE BREAK

35 _____ Composer _____
                                                    your name

▶ Compose a song that is shaped like the curved lines. Title and play your composition.

36 PENTATONIC SCALES

A Andante

B Andante

▶ Pentatonic scales consist of five notes. Two forms of the pentatonic scale are shown above.

37 GO FOR EXCELLENCE!

Korean Folk Song

▶ "Arirang" is based on a pentatonic scale.

| TEMPO | **Andantino** - Faster than **Andante**, but not as fast as **Moderato**. |

THIRTEEN STROKE ROLL

The thirteen stroke roll is a Rudiment.

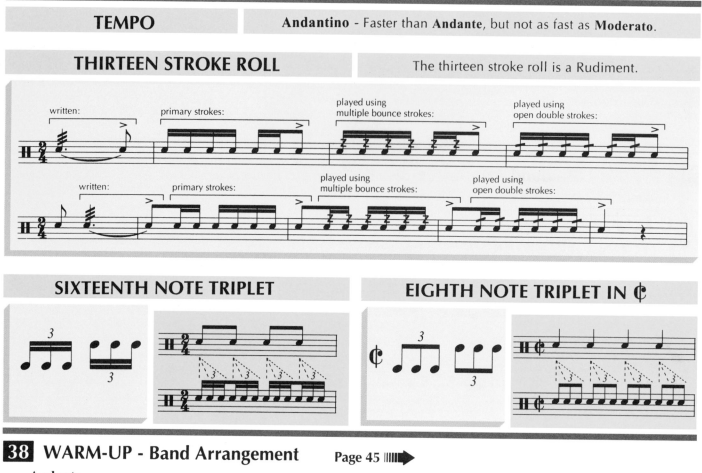

SIXTEEN NOTE TRIPLET

EIGHTH NOTE TRIPLET IN ¢

38 **WARM-UP - Band Arrangement** Page 45

Andante

mf

▶ This exercise may also be played on drum set.

39 **- Tacet** ▶ See "Mallets" page 10.

40 **TECHNIQUE BREAK**

Andantino

mf

41 **FOR SNARE DRUMS ONLY**

Andante

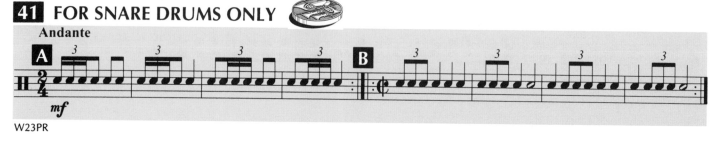

mf

D MINOR KEY SIGNATURE	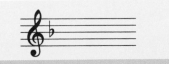	D minor has the same key signature as F major.
TEMPO		Andantino - Faster than Andante, but not as fast as Moderato.

38 WARM-UP - Band Arrangement

Andante

mf

39 D MINOR SCALE SKILL Page 44 ▶

Moderato

Natural Minor   Harmonic Minor

mf

Melodic Minor   Arpeggio   Chords

40 TECHNIQUE BREAK

Andantino

mf

41 FOR MALLETS ONLY

Moderato

mf

▶ Identify the intervals in measures 1-4 and 5-8 before you play.

FOUR MALLET TECHNIQUE

More advanced mallet percussion music often requires the percussionist to play three or four notes at one time. This necessitates the use of four mallet technique.

HOLDING THE MALLETS

STEP 1
In your right hand, hold a single mallet between your thumb and index finger as you normally would. Add a second mallet between your index and middle fingers. Place it so the butt end of the mallet extends slightly beyond the end of the mallet closest to your palm.

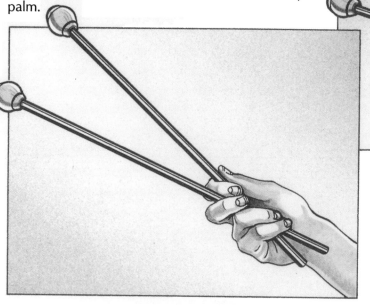

STEP 2
At the point where the mallets cross, grasp the mallet shafts with your ring and little fingers to form an anchor.

STEP 3
Repeat steps 1-2 with your left hand.

PLAYING USING FOUR MALLETS

STEP 1
With your palms down, use quick down-up strokes to strike the bars. Remain relaxed at all times.

STEP 2
To play larger intervals with one hand, place your thumb next to your index finger in the area between the crossed mallets. Spread your thumb and index finger apart to spread the mallets. Keep the mallet shafts crossed and anchored by your ring and little fingers.

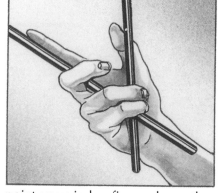

To play smaller intervals, squeeze the mallet shafts together with your little, ring, and middle fingers. Move your thumb outside of the area between the mallets and use it to help close the mallets. For very small intervals (seconds), point your index finger down the mallet shafts toward the mallet heads.

STEP 3
To become more comfortable with four mallet technique, hold four mallets even when practicing two mallet exercises. Generally, when using the grip described above, use the inside mallets ( ) to play two mallet passages (but feel free to experiment with other mallet combinations).

To play music that includes numerous skips and leaps (such as arpeggios), try using combinations of all four mallets.

FOUR MALLET STUDIES - FOR MALLETS ONLY

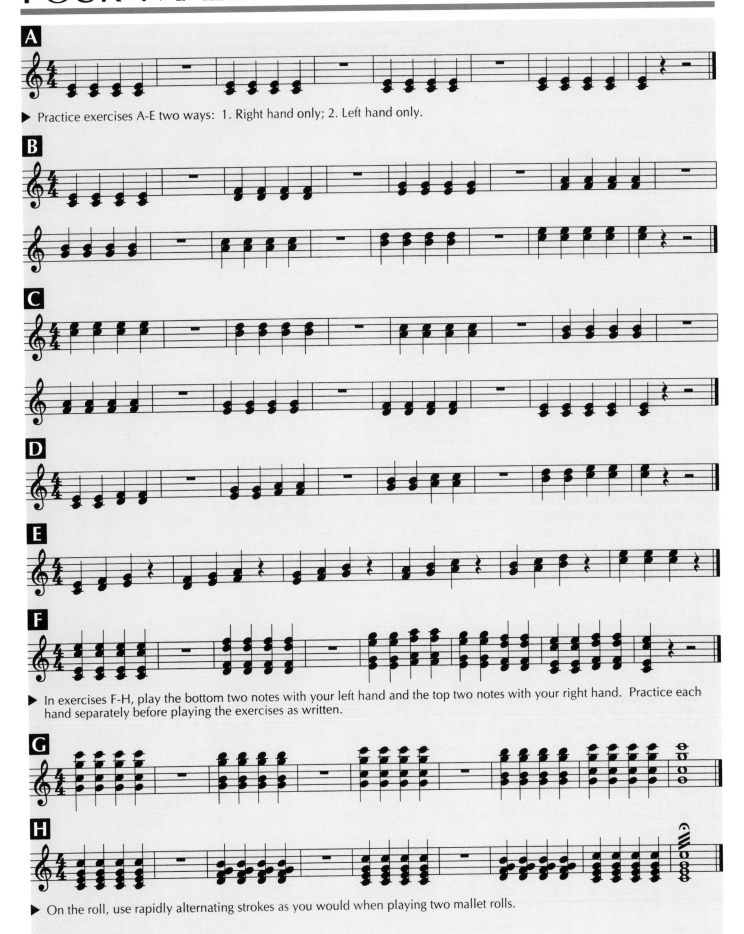

▶ Practice exercises A-E two ways: 1. Right hand only; 2. Left hand only.

▶ In exercises F-H, play the bottom two notes with your left hand and the top two notes with your right hand. Practice each hand separately before playing the exercises as written.

▶ On the roll, use rapidly alternating strokes as you would when playing two mallet rolls.

For additional four mallet practice:
▶ Play exercises 41 and 73 two additional ways: 1. Right hand only; 2. Left hand only.
▶ Hold four mallets as you play two mallet exercises.
▶ Transpose and play the exercises on this page in the keys of F, B♭, E♭, and A♭ major.
▶ Play the *Advanced Four Mallet Studies* on "Mallets" pages 46-47. Make them part of your daily practice routine.

SIXTEENTH REST

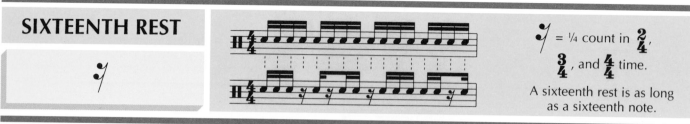

$\mathbf{\gamma}$ = ¼ count in $\frac{2}{4}$, $\frac{3}{4}$, and $\frac{4}{4}$ time.

A sixteenth rest is as long as a sixteenth note.

42 TINGA LAYO

West Indies Folk Song

Moderato

© M. Baron Co. Used by permission.

43 HWI NE YA HE

American Indian Song

Allegro

44 SIXTEENTH STUDY

Andantino

▶ Write in the counting and clap the rhythm before you play.

45 GO FOR EXCELLENCE!

French Canadian Folk Song

Allegretto

"Envoyons D'L'Avant, Nos Gens!"

SIXTEENTH REST

γ = ¼ count in 2/4, 3/4, and 4/4 time.

A sixteenth rest is as long as a sixteenth note.

42 TINGA LAYO   West Indies Folk Song

Moderato

mf

Fine   *D.C. al Fine*

© M. Baron Co. Used by permission.

43 HWI NE YA HE   American Indian Song

Allegro

f

44 SIXTEENTH STUDY

Andantino

mf

▶ Write in the counting and clap the rhythm before you play.

45 GO FOR EXCELLENCE!   French Canadian Folk Song

Allegretto

"Envoyons D'L'Avant, Nos Gens!"

mp

▶ Name the key in "Go For Excellence!" _____

THE MIDDLE AGES (400 - 1400)

DOTTED QUARTER REST	𝄽.	A dot after a rest adds half the value of the rest.

$$\text{𝄽} + \cdot = \text{𝄽} + \text{𝄾} = \text{𝄽}.$$

46 - **Tacet** ▶ See "Mallets" page 12.

47 DESCENDIT DE COELIS

Notre Dame Organum

▶ Play the B part using multiple bounce stroke rolls.

48 ESTAMPIE Page 45 ▬▬▶

Anonymous

49 SUMER IS ICUMEN IN

English Round

THE MIDDLE AGES (400 - 1400)

DOTTED QUARTER REST

A dot after a rest adds half the value of the rest.

46 CONFIRMA HOC

Plainsong

Con - fir - ma hoc De - us   quad o - pe - rá - tus es in no - bis

▶ Keep the eighth notes even at all times.

© G.I.A. Publications, Inc. Used by permission.

47 DESCENDIT DE COELIS

Notre Dame Organum

48 ESTAMPIE

Anonymous

49 SUMER IS ICUMEN IN

English Round

THE RENAISSANCE (1400 - 1600)

SINGLE RATAMACUE

The single ratamacue is a Rudiment.

50 D♭ MAJOR SCALE SKILL

Andantino

51 - Tacet ▶ See "Mallets" page 13.

52 TECHNIQUE BREAK

Andantino

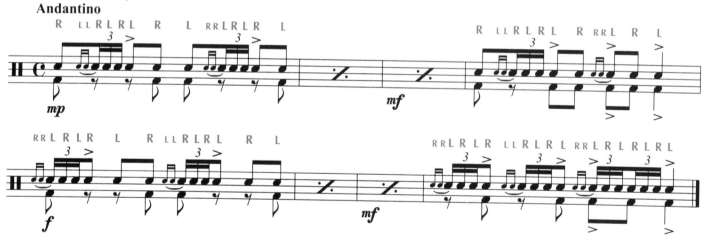

53 GO FOR EXCELLENCE!

Thoinot Arbeau (1520 - 1595)

"The Official Branle"

snares off

THE RENAISSANCE (1400 - 1600)

D♭ MAJOR KEY SIGNATURE		This key signature means play all B's as B flats, all E's as E flats, all A's as A flats, all D's as D flats, and all G's as G flats.

50 D♭ MAJOR SCALE SKILL Page 44 ▶

Andantino

f

Arpeggio

Chords

51 VOX DILECTI MEI - Band Arrangement

Palestrina (1525 - 1594)
arr. Bruce Pearson (b. 1942)

52 TECHNIQUE BREAK

Andantino

mp

mf

f

mf

53 GO FOR EXCELLENCE!

Thoinot Arbeau (1520 - 1595)

"The Official Branle"

DOUBLE RATAMACUE

The double ratamacue is a Rudiment.

SEVEN STROKE ROLL (TRIPLET PRIMARY STROKES)

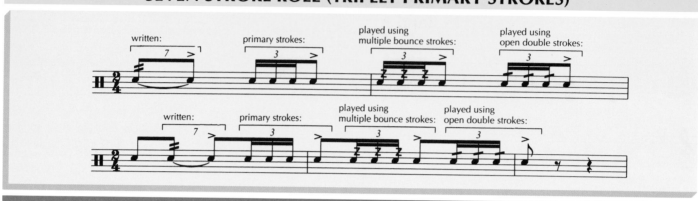

54 / **55** - Tacet   ▶ See "Mallets" page 14.

56 **TECHNIQUE BREAK**

57 **BERGERETTE SANS ROCHE**

Basse Danse
Tielman Susato (c. 1500 - c. 1561)

 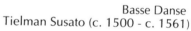

© MUSIKit Recorder, Roger and Carol Buckton, The Recorder Centre. Used by permission.

58 **FOR SNARE DRUMS ONLY**    **Page 45** ▰▰▰▶

▶ Play the seven stroke rolls using triplet primary strokes.

ENHARMONICS

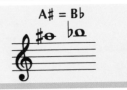

A# = Bb

54 OLD ONE HUNDREDTH - Band Arrangement

Louis Bourgeois (c. 1510 - c. 1561)
arr. Bruce Pearson (b. 1942)

55 NOW IS THE MONTH OF MAYING

Thomas Morley (1557 - 1602)

56 TECHNIQUE BREAK

Allegro

mf

57 BERGERETTE SANS ROCHE

Basse Danse
Tielman Susato (c. 1500 - c. 1561)

© MUSIKit Recorder, Roger and Carol Buckton, The Recorder Centre. Used by permission.

58 FOR MALLETS ONLY

Andantino   A#

mf

► Play the lower octave notes with your left hand and the upper octave notes with your right hand.

EARLE OF OXFORDS MARCHE

Band Arrangement

William Byrd (1543 - 1623)
arr. Bruce Pearson (b. 1942)

59 - **Tacet** ▶ See "Mallets" page 15.

60 **GO FOR EXCELLENCE!**

EARLE OF OXFORDS MARCHE

Band Arrangement

Bells

William Byrd (1543 - 1623)
arr. Bruce Pearson (b. 1942)

59

Arranger _____

your name

▶ Create fauxbourdon by writing a duet part a sixth below this Renaissance melody. Title your composition, and play the top part while a friend plays the bottom part.

60 GO FOR EXCELLENCE!

THE BAROQUE PERIOD (1600 - 1750)

TRIPLE RATAMACUE

The triple ratamacue is a Rudiment.

61 - Tacet ▶ See "Mallets" page 16.

62 TRUMPET TUNE

Henry Purcell (1659 - 1695)

Maestoso

63 LE PETIT RIEN

François Couperin (1668 - 1733)

Allegretto

64 FOR SNARE DRUMS ONLY

Moderato

Triple Ratamacue

THE BAROQUE PERIOD (1600 - 1750)

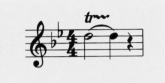

TRILL — A rapid alternation from the written note to the note above it in the key of the piece.

61 BALANCE BUILDER

62 TRUMPET TUNE

Henry Purcell (1659 - 1695)

Maestoso

63 LE PETIT RIEN

François Couperin (1668 - 1733)

Allegretto

64 FOR MALLETS ONLY

Allegro

▶ On the trills, move the mallets as rapidly as possible.

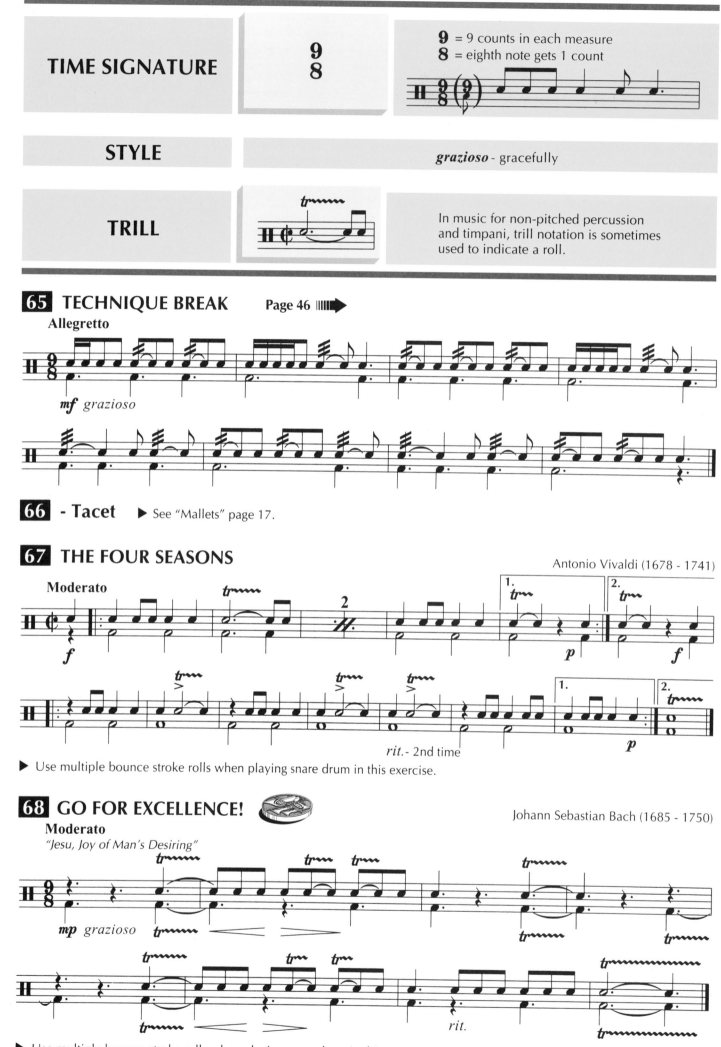

TIME SIGNATURE

$\frac{9}{8}$

9 = 9 counts in each measure
8 = eighth note gets 1 count

STYLE

grazioso - gracefully

TRILL

In music for non-pitched percussion and timpani, trill notation is sometimes used to indicate a roll.

65 **TECHNIQUE BREAK** Page 46

Allegretto

mf grazioso

66 - **Tacet** ▶ See "Mallets" page 17.

67 **THE FOUR SEASONS**

Antonio Vivaldi (1678 - 1741)

Moderato

f   *p*   *f*

rit.- 2nd time   *p*

▶ Use multiple bounce stroke rolls when playing snare drum in this exercise.

68 **GO FOR EXCELLENCE!**

Johann Sebastian Bach (1685 - 1750)

Moderato
"Jesu, Joy of Man's Desiring"

mp grazioso

rit.

▶ Use multiple bounce stroke rolls when playing snare drum in this exercise.

TIME SIGNATURE

$\frac{9}{8}$

9 = 9 counts in each measure
8 = eighth note gets 1 count

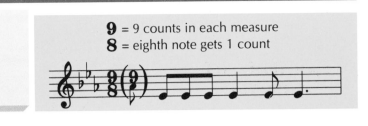

STYLE

grazioso - gracefully

65 TECHNIQUE BREAK

Allegretto

mf

grazioso

▶ Write in the counting and clap the rhythm before you play.

66 ALLEMANDE

Arcangelo Corelli (1653 - 1713)

Moderato

mf

rit. - 2nd time

▶ Be sure to trill up to E♭.

67 THE FOUR SEASONS

Antonio Vivaldi (1678 - 1741)

Moderato

f

1. *p* **2.** *f*

rit.- 2nd time *p*

68 GO FOR EXCELLENCE!

Johann Sebastian Bach (1685 - 1750)

Moderato

"Jesu, Joy of Man's Desiring"

mp grazioso

rit.

PARADIDDLE-DIDDLE

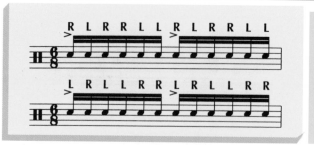

The paradiddle-diddle is a Rudiment.

69 - **Tacet** ▶ See "Mallets" page 18.

70 **HORNPIPE FROM "WATER MUSIC SUITE"**

George Frideric Handel (1685 - 1759)

71 **TECHNIQUE BREAK**

72 **FANTASIA CHROMATICA**

Johann Sebastian Bach (1685 - 1750)

73 **FOR SNARE DRUMS ONLY**

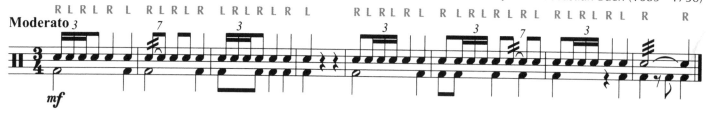

74 ARTICULATION ADVENTURE

Moderato

mf

▶ Write in the counting and clap the rhythm before you play.

75 MINUETTO

Domenico Scarlatti (1685 - 1757)

Allegretto

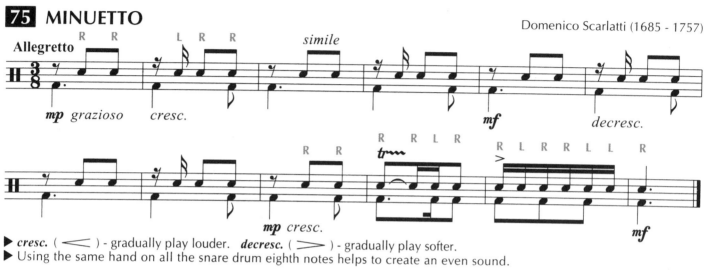

mp grazioso   *cresc.*   *simile*   *mf*   *decresc.*

mp cresc.   *mf*

▶ *cresc.* (⟨) - gradually play louder.   *decresc.* (⟩) - gradually play softer.
▶ Using the same hand on all the snare drum eighth notes helps to create an even sound.

76 PASSEPIED

Georg Philipp Telemann (1681 - 1767)

Allegro

f - 1st time
p - 2nd time

f - 1st time
p - 2nd time

© Southern Music Co. Used by permission.

77 GO FOR EXCELLENCE!

George Frideric Handel (1685 - 1759)

Andantino

"Siciliana from Music for the Royal Fireworks"

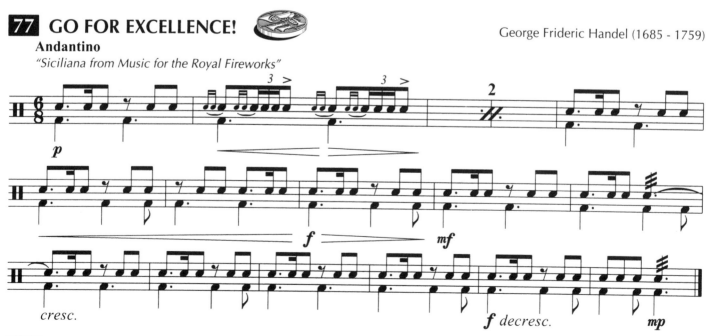

p

cresc.   *f*   *mf*   *f decresc.*   *mp*

SIXTEENTH NOTES IN 3/8, 6/8, & 9/8 TIME

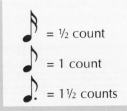

♪ = ½ count

♪ = 1 count

♪. = 1½ counts

A single sixteenth note is half as long as an eighth note.

74 ARTICULATION ADVENTURE

Moderato

mf

▶ Write in the counting and clap the rhythm before you play.

75 MINUETTO

Domenico Scarlatti (1685 - 1757)

Allegretto

mp grazioso   *cresc.*   *mf*   *decresc.*

mp cresc.   *mf*

▶ **cresc.** (<) - gradually play louder.   **decresc.** (>) - gradually play softer.

76 PASSEPIED

Georg Philipp Telemann (1681 - 1767)

Allegro

f - 1st time
p - 2nd time

f - 1st time
p - 2nd time

© Southern Music Co. Used by permission.

77 GO FOR EXCELLENCE!

George Frideric Handel (1685 - 1759)

Andantino

"Siciliana from Music for the Royal Fireworks"

p legato

f > *mf*

cresc.   *f decresc.*   *mp*

78 TECHNIQUE BREAK

Andante

▶ Use flam paradiddles when playing the eighth note groups.

REJOUISSANCE
from Music for the Royal Fireworks
Band Arrangement

George Frideric Handel (1685 - 1759)
arr. Bruce Pearson (b. 1942)

Moderato

78 **TECHNIQUE BREAK**

▶ Name the key in "Technique Break." _____

REJOUISSANCE
from Music for the Royal Fireworks
Band Arrangement

Xylophone

George Frideric Handel (1685 - 1759)
arr. Bruce Pearson (b. 1942)

THE CLASSICAL PERIOD (1750 - 1820)

TEMPO Larghetto - not as slow as **Largo**

STYLE *dolce* - sweetly

GRACE NOTE

A small-sized note played just before the note to which it is attached. Flams, drags, and four stroke ruffs all contain grace notes.

FOUR STROKE RUFF

ARTICULATION

staccato (dot placed above or below note) - play short and detached

79 THEME FROM PIANO SONATA NO. 2

Wolfgang Amadeus Mozart (1756 - 1791)

80 GERMAN DANCE

Franz Joseph Haydn (1732 - 1809)

81 TECHNIQUE BREAK

Page 46

82 GO FOR EXCELLENCE!

Ludwig van Beethoven (1770 - 1827)

"Sonatina"

THE CLASSICAL PERIOD (1750 - 1820)

GRACE NOTE		TEMPO	STYLE
A small-sized note played just before the note to which it is attached.		**Larghetto** - not as slow as **Largo**	*dolce* - sweetly

79 **THEME FROM PIANO SONATA NO. 2** Wolfgang Amadeus Mozart (1756 - 1791)

Larghetto

▶ Try playing both octaves at the same time.

80 **GERMAN DANCE** Page 44 ▕▕▕▶ Franz Joseph Haydn (1732 - 1809)

Allegretto

81 **TECHNIQUE BREAK**

Moderato

82 **GO FOR EXCELLENCE!**   Ludwig van Beethoven (1770 - 1827)

Larghetto

BINARY FORM	AB	Music that has two different sections.

FLAM PARADIDDLE-DIDDLE		The flam paradiddle-diddle is a Rudiment.

83 - **Tacet** ▶ See "Mallets" page 22.

84 RUSSIAN FOLK SONG

Ludwig van Beethoven (1770 - 1827)

Allegro

Section A

85 TECHNIQUE BREAK

Andante

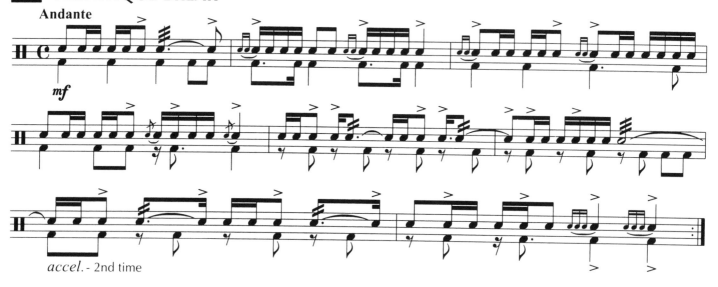

accel. - 2nd time

86 FOR SNARE DRUMS ONLY

Moderato

BINARY FORM	AB	Music that has two different sections.

STYLE		*simile* - Continue playing in the same manner.

Franz Joseph Haydn (1732 - 1809)
arr. Bruce Pearson (b. 1942)

83 AUSTRIAN HYMN - Band Arrangement

Andante

84 RUSSIAN FOLK SONG

Ludwig van Beethoven (1770 - 1827)

Allegro

85 TECHNIQUE BREAK

accel. - 2nd time

86 FOR MALLETS ONLY   Page 44 ▶

▶ Be sure that the second stroke of each double sticking (the rebound) is the same dynamic as the first.

TERNARY FORM

ABA

The A section is followed by the B section, and then the A section is played again.

87 SCOTCH DANCE

Ludwig van Beethoven (1770 - 1827)

Allegretto

▶ Name the form used in "Scotch Dance." _____

88 TECHNIQUE BREAK

Rodolphe Kreutzer (1766 - 1831)

Moderato

89 GO FOR EXCELLENCE!

Wolfgang Amadeus Mozart (1756 - 1791)

Moderato

"Theme from Symphony No. 40"

TERNARY FORM

ABA

The A section is followed by the B section, and then the A section is played again.

87 SCOTCH DANCE

Ludwig van Beethoven (1770 - 1827)

▶ Name the form used in "Scotch Dance." _____

88 TECHNIQUE BREAK

Rodolphe Kreutzer (1766 - 1831)

89 GO FOR EXCELLENCE!

Wolfgang Amadeus Mozart (1756 - 1791)

"Theme from Symphony No. 40"

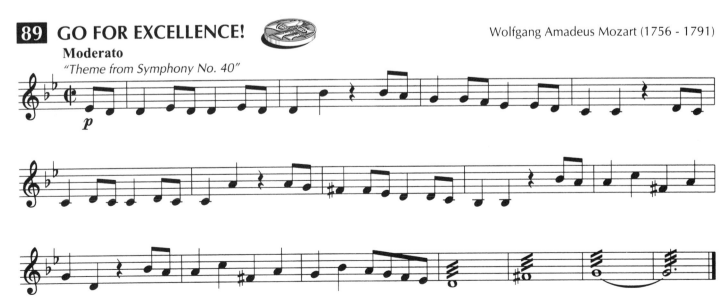

RONDO FORM

ABACA

The main section A returns several times and alternates with other sections.

90 - **Tacet** ▶ See "Mallets" page 24.

RONDO
Band Arrangement

Franz Joseph Haydn (1732 - 1809)
arr. Bruce Pearson (b. 1942)

Allegretto

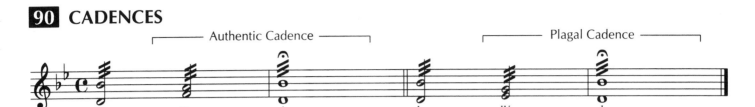

RONDO FORM

ABACA

The main section A returns several times and alternates with other sections.

90 CADENCES

RONDO

Band Arrangement

Franz Joseph Haydn (1732 - 1809)
arr. Bruce Pearson (b. 1942)

THE ROMANTIC PERIOD (1820 - 1900)

91 - Tacet ▶ See "Mallets" page 25.

92 F MINOR SCALE SKILL

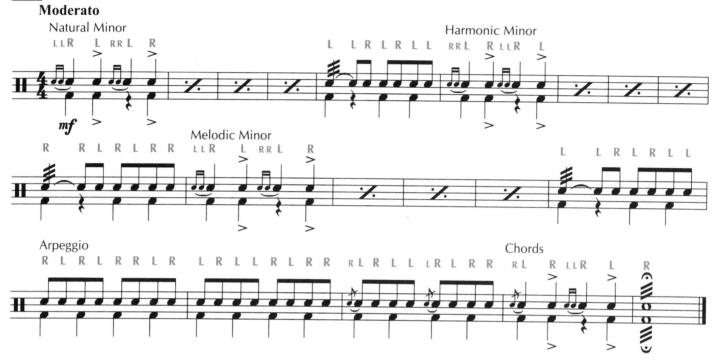

93 TECHNIQUE BREAK

▶ End the dotted half note rolls when the rest of the band cuts off.

94 GO FOR EXCELLENCE!

Johannes Brahms (1833 - 1897)

Allegretto
"Hungarian Dance No. 5"

▶ To ensure an even sound, use the same hand to play all the snare drum quarter notes.

THE ROMANTIC PERIOD (1820 - 1900)

F MINOR KEY SIGNATURE

F minor has the same key signature as **A♭ major**.

91 CAST THY BURDEN FROM "ELIJAH" - Band Arrangement

Felix Mendelssohn (1809 - 1847)
arr. Bruce Pearson (b. 1942)

Largo
Marimba

92 F MINOR SCALE SKILL   Page 44

Moderato

Natural Minor   Harmonic Minor

Melodic Minor   Arpeggio   Chords

93 TECHNIQUE BREAK

Moderato   Fine

D. C. al Fine

94 GO FOR EXCELLENCE!

Johannes Brahms (1833 - 1897)

Allegretto
"Hungarian Dance No. 5"

TIME SIGNATURE

6/4

6 = 6 counts in each measure
4 = quarter note gets 1 count

DAL SEGNO AL CODA (D.S. AL CODA)

Go back to the segno sign (𝄋) and play until the coda sign. When you reach the coda sign, skip to the **Coda.**

95 SCHEHERAZADE

Nicolai Rimsky-Korsakov (1844 - 1908)

Andantino 𝄋

p grazioso

to Coda ⊕

mp

D. S. al Coda

⊕ Coda

rit. *pp*

96 LAUGHING SONG FROM "DIE FLEDERMAUS"

Johann Strauss, Jr. (1825 - 1899)

Allegretto

mp

▶ Write in the counting and clap the rhythm before you play.

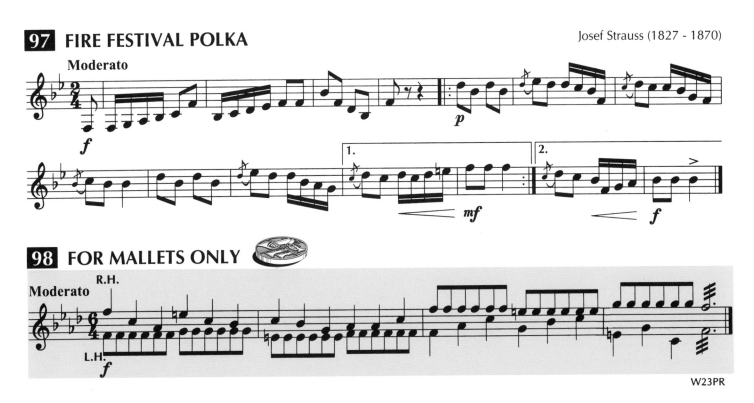

97 FIRE FESTIVAL POLKA

Josef Strauss (1827 - 1870)

Moderato

f

p

1.

mf

2.

f

98 FOR MALLETS ONLY

Moderato

R.H.

L.H.

f

TIME SIGNATURE

$\frac{5}{4}$

5 = 5 counts in each measure
4 = quarter note gets 1 count

STYLE

sostenuto - sustained

99 TECHNIQUE BREAK

Moderato

mf

▶ Write in the counting and clap the rhythm before you play.

100 G MAJOR SCALE SKILL

Andante

mf

Arpeggio

Chords

101 PILGRIMS CHORUS FROM "TANNHAUSER"

Richard Wagner (1813 - 1883)

Andante

mp *sostenuto*

cresc.

f

mp *f*

mp

102 GO FOR EXCELLENCE!

Modeste Mussorgsky (1839 - 1881)

Maestoso

"Promenade from Pictures at an Exhibition"

f sostenuto

rit. *ff*

TIME SIGNATURE	$\frac{5}{4}$	G MAJOR KEY SIGNATURE		STYLE

5 = 5 counts in each measure
4 = quarter note gets 1 count

This key signature means play all F's as F sharps.

sostenuto - sustained

99 TECHNIQUE BREAK

Moderato

mf

▶ Write in the counting and clap the rhythm before you play.

100 G MAJOR SCALE SKILL

Page 44 ◗◗◗➡

F#   G

Andante

mf

Arpeggio

Chords

101 PILGRIMS CHORUS FROM "TANNHAUSER"

Richard Wagner (1813 - 1883)

Andante

mp *sostenuto*

cresc.   *f*   *mp*   *f*   ▬▬▬▶ *mp*

1.

2.

102 GO FOR EXCELLENCE!

Modeste Mussorgsky (1839 - 1881)

Maestoso

"Promenade from Pictures at an Exhibition"

f *sostenuto*

rit.   *ff*

W23PR

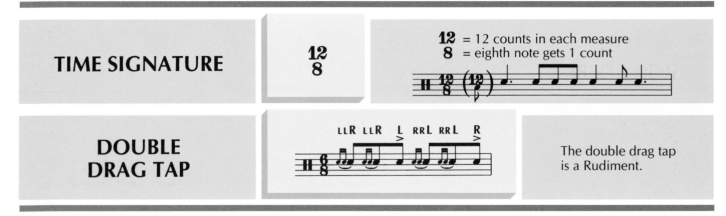

TIME SIGNATURE

$\frac{12}{8}$

12 = 12 counts in each measure
8 = eighth note gets 1 count

DOUBLE DRAG TAP

The double drag tap is a Rudiment.

103 ARTICULATION ADVENTURE

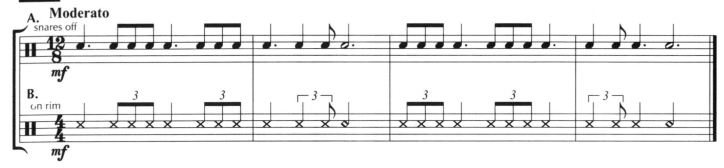

▶ Write in the counting and clap the rhythm before you play.

104 TECHNIQUE BREAK

Carl Czerny (1791 - 1857)

105 - Tacet ▶ See "Mallets" page 28.

106 FOR SNARE DRUMS ONLY

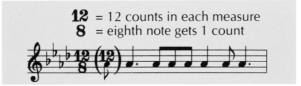

TIME SIGNATURE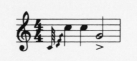

12 = 12 counts in each measure
8 = eighth note gets 1 count

DYNAMICS

sforzando (sfz) - accented

GLISSANDO
(gliss.)

A continuous slide from one note to another.

103 ARTICULATION ADVENTURE

▶ Write in the counting and clap the rhythm before you play.

104 TECHNIQUE BREAK

Carl Czerny (1791 - 1857)

105 THE WILD HORSEMAN

Robert Schumann (1810 - 1856)

▶ Line A is in the key of G minor. On line B, write in the melody a whole step lower to transpose to the key of F minor. Play both lines.

106 FOR MALLETS ONLY

Page 45 ▕▐▶

▶ On the glissandos, slide one mallet over the natural bars, and strike the ending note with the other mallet. The glissandos should be played before the beat.

WALTZ
from Waltz Op. 39, No. 15
Band Arrangement

Johannes Brahms (1833 - 1897)
arr. Chris Salerno (b. 1968)

107 TECHNIQUE BREAK

▶ Ask your teacher to explain the Moeller technique, and use it when playing this exercise.
▶ Try playing this exercise using the following patterns:

108 GO FOR EXCELLENCE!

Peter Ilyich Tchaikovsky (1840 - 1893)

Andante
"Theme from Symphony No. 5"

▶ Use multiple bounce stroke rolls when playing snare drum in this exercise.

STYLE | *cantabile* - in a singing style

ENHARMONICS

WALTZ
from Waltz Op. 39, No. 15
Band Arrangement

Xylophone

Johannes Brahms (1833 - 1897)
arr. Chris Salerno (b. 1968)

107 **TECHNIQUE BREAK** Page 45 ▶

108 **GO FOR EXCELLENCE!**

Peter Ilyich Tchaikovsky (1840 - 1893)

"Theme from Symphony No. 5"

20th CENTURY ART MUSIC

FIFTEEN STROKE ROLL

The fifteen stroke roll is a Rudiment.

109 A MINOR SCALE SKILL

Moderato

▶ This exercise may be played on drum set.

110 PAVANE

Gabriel Fauré (1845 - 1924)

Andantino

mp *cantabile*

pp

111 / 112 - Tacet ▶ See "Mallets" page 30.

113 THE SUNKEN CATHEDRAL - Band Arrangement

Impressionism Example
Claude Debussy (1862 - 1918)
arr. Chuck Elledge (b. 1961)

Maestoso

ff

▶ In this piece, the woodwinds and brass demonstrate a technique called planing, where all notes of a chord move the same direction. This is also called parallel motion.
▶ Play the B.D. part using two mallets.

20th CENTURY ART MUSIC

| A MINOR KEY SIGNATURE |  | **A minor** has the same key signature as **C major**. |

109 A MINOR SCALE SKILL Page 45 ▸

110 PAVANE

Gabriel Fauré (1845 - 1924)

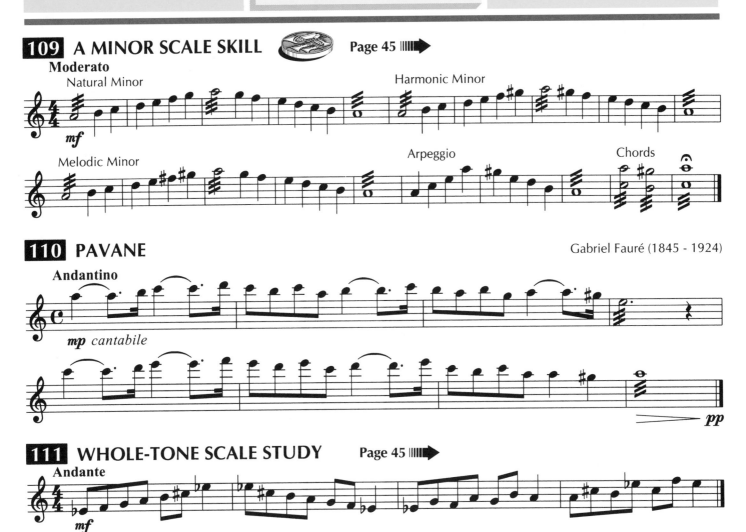

111 WHOLE-TONE SCALE STUDY Page 45 ▸

▶ A whole-tone scale consists of only whole steps.

112 EXCERPT FROM "PRELUDE TO THE AFTERNOON OF A FAUN"

Impressionism Example
Claude Debussy (1862 - 1918)

▶ This piece is based on a whole-tone scale. In measure 6, be sure to trill up a whole step.

113 THE SUNKEN CATHEDRAL - Band Arrangement

Impressionism Example
Claude Debussy (1862 - 1918)
arr. Chuck Elledge (b. 1961)

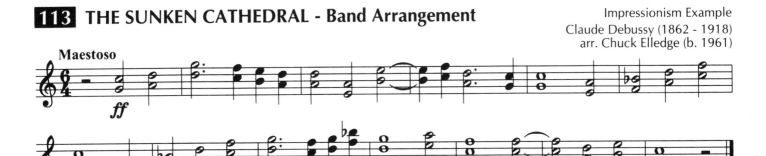

▶ This piece demonstrates a technique called planing, where all notes of a chord move the same direction. This is also called parallel motion.

ASYMMETRICAL METERS

Meters or time signatures with an uneven number of eighth notes (usually $\frac{3}{8}$, $\frac{5}{8}$, or $\frac{7}{8}$).

DYNAMICS

sforzando (sfz) - accented

114 FOLK MELODY A LA BÉLA BARTÓK (1881 - 1945)

Nationalism Example
Stephen Foster (1826 - 1864)
arr. Chris Salerno (b. 1968)

Allegretto
"Oh! Susanna"

115 ODE TO IGOR STRAVINSKY (1882 - 1971) - **Band Arrangement**

Primitivism Example
Chris Salerno (b. 1968)

Moderato

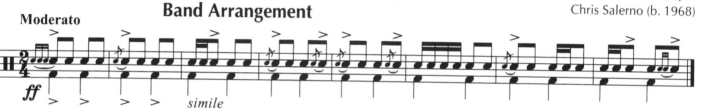

116 TECHNIQUE BREAK

Moderato

117 GO FOR EXCELLENCE!

Claude Debussy (1862 - 1918)

Allegro
"Golliwog's Cake Walk from Children's Corner"

ASYMMETRICAL METERS

Meters or time signatures with an uneven number of eighth notes (usually $\frac{3}{8}$, $\frac{5}{8}$, or $\frac{7}{8}$).

114 FOLK MELODY A LA BÉLA BARTÓK (1881 - 1945)

Nationalism Example
Stephen Foster (1826 - 1864)
arr. Chris Salerno (b. 1968)

Allegretto
"Oh! Susanna"

115 ODE TO IGOR STRAVINSKY (1882 - 1971) - Band Arrangement

Primitivism Example
Chris Salerno (b. 1968)

Moderato

116 TECHNIQUE BREAK

▶ Write in the counting and clap the rhythm before you play.

117 GO FOR EXCELLENCE!

Claude Debussy (1862 - 1918)

Allegro
"Golliwog's Cake Walk from Children's Corner"

DYNAMICS

forte-piano (fp) - loud, then immediately soft

ELEVEN STROKE ROLL

The eleven stroke roll is a Rudiment.

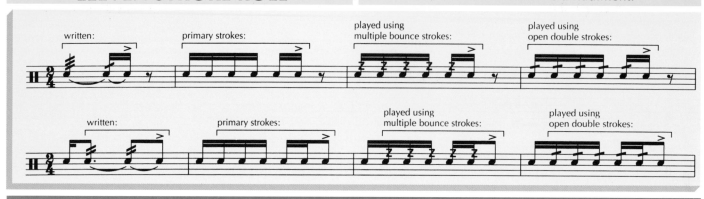

118 **HOMAGE TO ANTON WEBERN (1883 - 1945)**

Twelve-tone Example
Chris Salerno (b. 1968)

Moderato

▶ Use multiple bounce stroke rolls when playing this exercise.

119 / **120** - **Tacet**   ▶ See "Mallets" page 32.

121 **FOR SNARE DRUMS ONLY**

Moderato

Twelve-tone Example
Chris Salerno (b. 1968)

118 HOMAGE TO ANTON WEBERN (1883 - 1945)

Tone Row

▶ Notice that the tone row uses all twelve notes of the chromatic scale once.

Moderato

119 TONE ROW

Moderato

120 _____   Composer _____
                                                        your name

▶ Compose a twelve-tone composition. Title and play your composition.

121 FOR MALLETS ONLY   Page 45 ▶

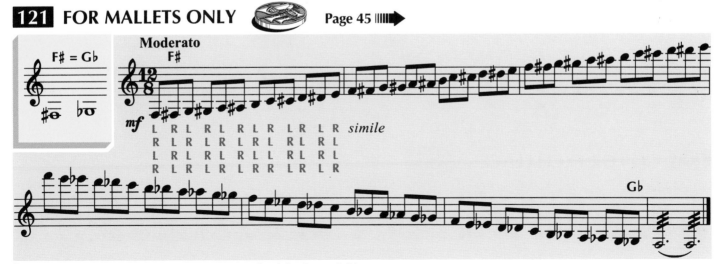

▶ Practice this chromatic exercise using each of the four sticking patterns.

WAR
from The Four Horsemen
Band Arrangement

Andrew Boysen, Jr. (b. 1968)

122 TRIBUTE TO CHARLES IVES (1874 - 1954)

Bitonal Example
Stephen Foster (1826 - 1864)
arr. Chris Salerno (b. 1968)

Allegretto
"Camptown Races"

123 GO FOR EXCELLENCE!

Moderato

WAR
from The Four Horsemen
Band Arrangement

Andrew Boysen, Jr. (b. 1968)

Xylophone

122 TRIBUTE TO CHARLES IVES (1874 - 1954)

Bitonal Example
Stephen Foster (1826 - 1864)
arr. Chris Salerno (b. 1968)

123 GO FOR EXCELLENCE!

W23PR

20th Century Pop Music

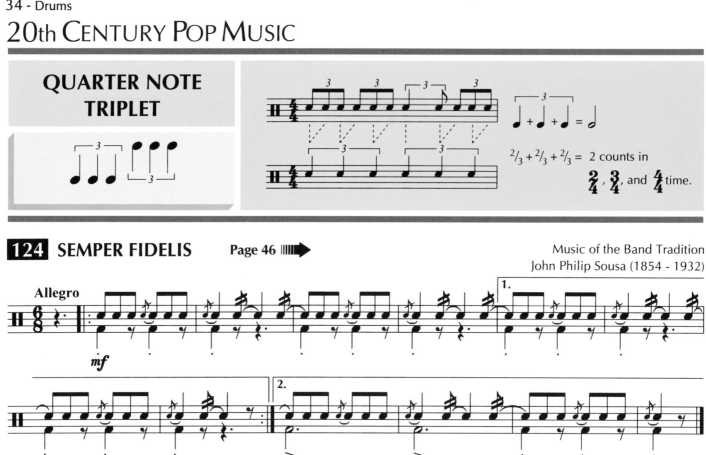

QUARTER NOTE TRIPLET

$$\frac{2}{3} + \frac{2}{3} + \frac{2}{3} = 2 \text{ counts in}$$

$\frac{2}{4}$, $\frac{3}{4}$, and $\frac{4}{4}$ time.

124 **SEMPER FIDELIS** Page 46 ▶

Music of the Band Tradition
John Philip Sousa (1854 - 1932)

125 **THE EASY WINNERS**

Ragtime Example
Scott Joplin (1868 - 1917)

126 **TRIPLETS, TRIPLETS, TRIPLETS**

127 **TECHNIQUE BREAK**

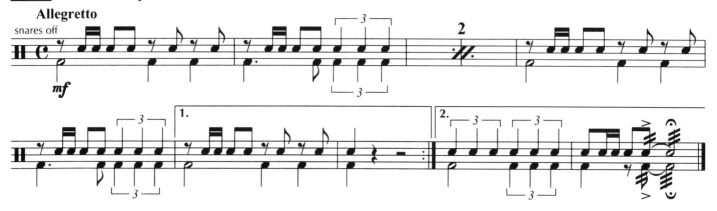

20th CENTURY POP MUSIC

QUARTER NOTE TRIPLET

124 SEMPER FIDELIS

Music of the Band Tradition
John Philip Sousa (1854 - 1932)

125 THE EASY WINNERS

Ragtime Example
Scott Joplin (1868 - 1917)

126 TRIPLETS, TRIPLETS, TRIPLETS

127 TECHNIQUE BREAK

▶ Write in the counting and clap the rhythm before you play.

| STYLE | *Swing* - ♪♪ played as ⌐³¬ ♩♪ | *Ride* - a steady repetitive pattern, usually played on suspended cymbal or hi-hat. |

PLAYING THE SNARE DRUM WITH BRUSHES

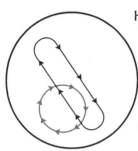

Hold a brush in each hand, using your normal grip. With your left hand, slide the brush wires on the drum head using steady circular swish motions. Two possible motions are shown in the diagram. (At medium tempos when using the black motion, create half the circle on each beat; when using the green motion, create the entire circle on each beat.) With your right hand, tap the brush wires on the head, striking the head in an area which does not interfere with the motion of your left hand. Also practice these techniques with the roles of your hands reversed.

128 SWINGING BLUES SCALE

▶ This exercise may be played on drum set.

129 SWINGING BLUES CHORD PROGRESSION (Arpeggios)

Page 47 ▦▶

▶ This exercise may be played on drum set.

130 BLUES CHORD ACCOMPANIMENT - Band Arrangement /
131 TIN ROOF BLUES / 132 GO FOR EXCELLENCE! *"Blues for a Fat Cat"*

▶ This exercise may be played on drum set. Play the "stems down" S.D. part by sliding the brush on the head, making steady circular motions. Play the "stems up" S.D. part by tapping the brush on the head.

▶ Ask your teacher to explain other techniques that may be used when playing with brushes.

STYLE

Swing - ♪♪ played as ♩³♪

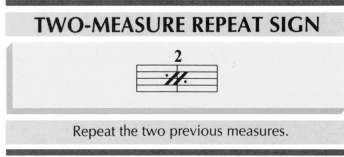

TWO-MEASURE REPEAT SIGN

Repeat the two previous measures.

128 SWINGING BLUES SCALE   Page 45 ▶

129 SWINGING BLUES CHORD PROGRESSION (Arpeggios)

130 BLUES CHORD ACCOMPANIMENT - Band Arrangement

▶ This exercise can be played with 131 and 132.

131 TIN ROOF BLUES   Page 45 ▶   Traditional Blues Example

132 GO FOR EXCELLENCE!

"Blues for a Fat Cat"

STYLE	***ad libitum (ad lib.)*** - with liberties; improvise within the boundaries of the music

133 '55 T-BIRD

1950s Rock and Roll Example
Kevin Daley (b. 1957)

Moderato

▶ This exercise may be played on drum set.

134 RIGHT ON   Page 47 ▶

1970s Rock Example
Kevin Daley (b. 1957)

Allegretto

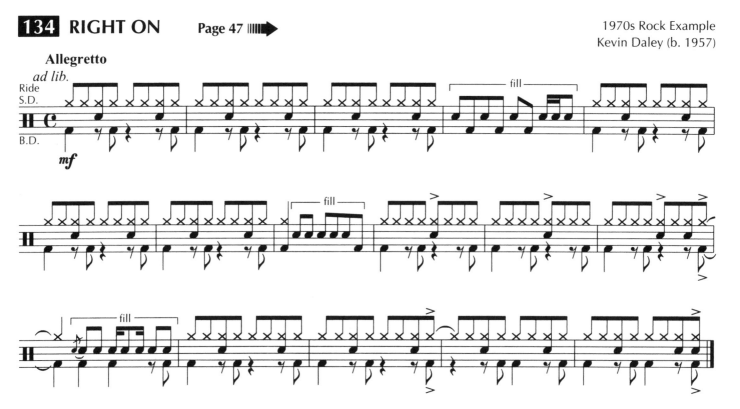

▶ This exercise may be played on drum set.

133 **'55 T-BIRD**

1950s Rock and Roll Example
Kevin Daley (b. 1957)

134 **RIGHT ON**

1970s Rock Example
Kevin Daley (b. 1957)

▶ Write in the counting and clap the rhythm before you play.

JAMBALAYA JAMMIN'
Band Arrangement

James "Red" McLeod (b. 1912)

► This part may be played on drum set.

JAMBALAYA JAMMIN'
Band Arrangement

Bells
Xylophone

James "Red" McLeod (b. 1912)

▶ This part should be played by two percussionists.

SCALE STUDIES

1 **B♭ MAJOR SCALE**

2 **G HARMONIC MINOR SCALE**

3 **E♭ MAJOR SCALE**

4 **C HARMONIC MINOR SCALE**

SCALE STUDIES

5 **F MAJOR SCALE**

6 **D HARMONIC MINOR SCALE**

7 **A♭ MAJOR SCALE**

8 **F HARMONIC MINOR SCALE**

SCALE STUDIES

9 C MAJOR SCALE

10 A HARMONIC MINOR SCALE

11 D♭ MAJOR SCALE

12 G MAJOR SCALE

13 CHROMATIC SCALE

RHYTHM STUDIES

RHYTHM STUDIES

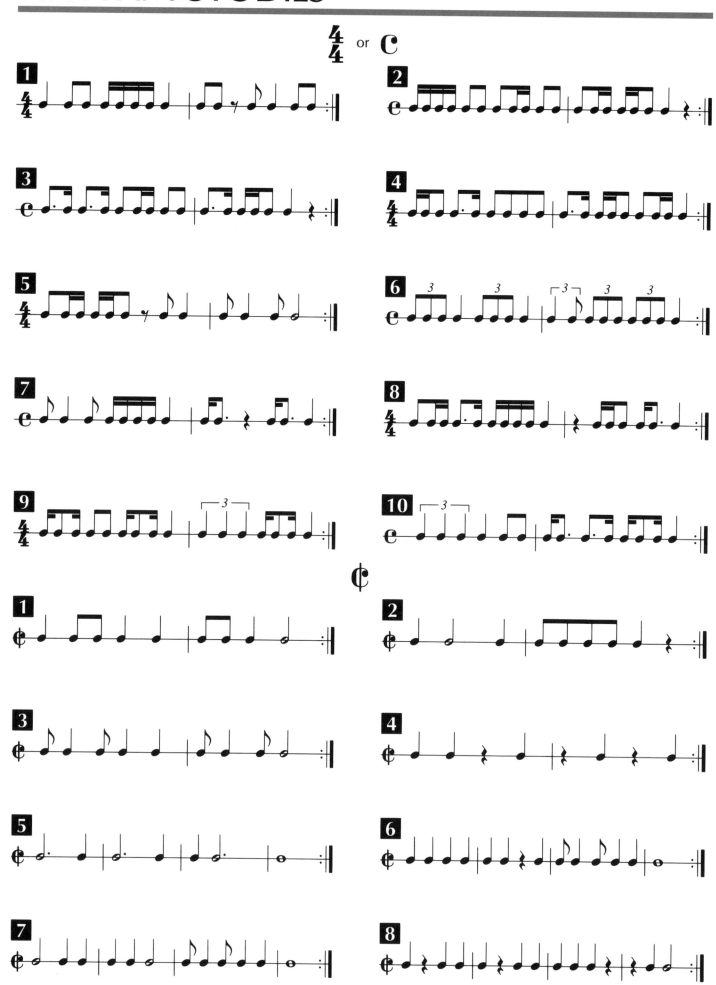

RHYTHM STUDIES

EXCELLERATORS - FOR DRUMS ONLY

ROLLS IN ⅜ & 6/8 (fast tempos)

FIVE STROKE ROLL

SEVEN STROKE ROLL

▶ Play each pattern several times without stopping. Try a variety of tempos and dynamics.

▶ Play this exercise two ways: 1. Allegro, playing the rolls as shown at the top of the page; 2. Andante, playing the rolls as shown on "Drums" page 6.

▶ Play this exercise two ways: 1. Allegro, playing the rolls as shown at the top of the page; 2. Andante, playing the rolls as shown on "Drums" page 6.

EXCELLERATORS - FOR DRUMS ONLY

▶ Play each pattern several times without stopping. Try a variety of tempos and dynamics.

A piece of music is made up of short musical thoughts called phrases. A fill is a rhythmic figure often played at the end of a phrase to lead into a new phrase. Percussionists are frequently required to play fills, especially when performing drum set or drum set style parts.

Use the following rhythms and five-step procedure to develop your ability to create and perform fills:

1. Repeatedly play rhythm F on a single surface (snare, tom, bass drum, or cymbal).
2. In the context of the following four measure phrase, play rhythm F on a single surface. (Play the fill where you see slashes in the music.)

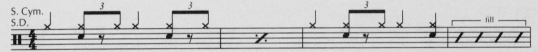

3. Divide rhythm F between any two surfaces. Experiment with different combinations of surfaces, and use logical stickings.
4. Divide rhythm F between any three surfaces, then four, then five, etc.
5. Repeat steps 1-4 with rhythms G-M.

▶ Practice this exercise two ways: 1. At an Andante tempo; 2. At an Allegro tempo. Interpret the rolls in a way appropriate to each tempo.

▶ Use the top stickings the first time through and the bottom stickings the second time through.

⫸ EXCELLERATORS - FOR DRUMS ONLY

SINGLE FLAMMED MILL

PATAFLAFLA

SWISS ARMY TRIPLET

INVERTED FLAM TAP

The single flammed mill, pataflafla, Swiss Army triplet, and inverted flam tap are Rudiments.

▶ Practice this example two ways: 1. At an Andante tempo; 2. At an Allegro tempo.

▶ EXCELLERATORS - FOR DRUMS ONLY

THE DRUM SET - BASS DRUM AND HI-HAT

PLAYING THE BASS DRUM WITH YOUR FOOT

Place your right foot on the pedal board, with your heel on the heel plate. Using your heel as a pivot point, quickly move the ball of your foot in a down/up motion that causes the beater to strike the head and rebound. Both the ball of your foot and your heel should remain on the pedal board throughout the entire stroke.

PLAYING THE HI-HAT WITH YOUR FOOT

Place your left foot on the hi-hat pedal board, with your heel on the heel plate.

Close the hi-hat by pushing down with the ball of your foot while lifting your heel.

Open the hi-hat by bringing your heel back to the heel plate, allowing the pedal to spring back up. When opened and closed repeatedly, your foot will look and feel like it is rocking back and forth.

PLAYING THE HI-HAT WITH YOUR HAND

To play the hi-hat with your right hand, cross your right hand over your left.
To play the hi-hat with your left hand, your hands remain uncrossed.

Depending on the desired sound, either strike the top cymbal halfway between the bell and the edge with the bead of the stick, or strike the edge of the top cymbal with the shoulder of the stick. As you play, the hi-hat may either remain closed, or may be opened and closed ad lib. or as directed by the music.

Use both hands to play fast or rhythmically active hi-hat parts.

To learn about other important drum set techniques, see *Drum Sessions Book 1* (151DCT) and *Drum Sessions Book 2* (152DCT) by Peter O'Gorman.
(Neil A. Kjos Music Company, publisher).

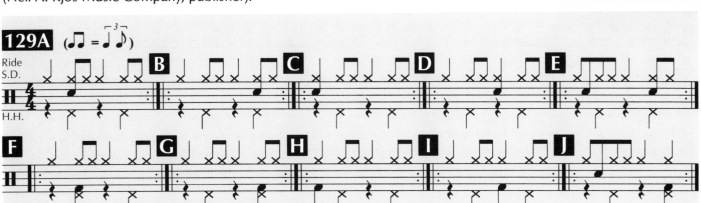

▶ Jazz rides like the one in these patterns are usually played on suspended cymbal.

▶ Eighth note rides may be played on suspended cymbal or hi-hat. Practice the ride in these patterns four ways: 1. Right hand on S. Cym.; 2. Left hand on S. Cym. (if your drum kit set-up includes a cymbal on the left side of the kit); 3. Right hand on hi-hat; 4. Left hand on hi-hat.

▶ For additional practice, play *Standard of Excellence* Book 2 Drum Excellerators 45, 57, 72, 77, 81, 101, 111, and 113 on drum set, adding a hi-hat part played by the left foot on beats 2 and 4, or all four beats, of each pattern.

▣▣▶ EXCELLERATORS - FOR MALLETS ONLY

11A

▶ The note labels designate the major chord being played.

B

▶ The note labels designate the minor chord being played.
  * Fb = E; Bbb = A; Cb = B

39

50

▦▶ EXCELLERATORS - FOR MALLETS ONLY

80 **Allegretto**
"Sonatina in G Major"

Muzio Clementi (1752 - 1832)

▶ Practice slowly at first and gradually build up speed.

86

L L R R *simile*

R R L L *simile*

▶ For additional practice, play TECHNIQUE BREAKS 2, 21, 40, 52, 81, and 85 again. This time, play all eighth notes as two sixteenth notes (♪ = ♫). Use double strokes for the sixteenth note pairs.

92

100

EXCELLERATORS - FOR MALLETS ONLY

106 **Allegro**
"Thunder and Lightning Polka"

Johann Strauss, Jr.

▶ Practice slowly at first and gradually build up speed.

107

▶ The note labels designate the major chord being played. For additional practice, repeat each chord two, three, or four times before moving on to the next chord.

109 **Largo**

111A

B

▶ Play each pattern several times without stopping. Try a variety of stickings.

121A

▶ Notice how one hand remains on D while the other moves away from D chromatically.

▦▶ EXCELLERATORS - FOR MALLETS ONLY

121B

R R L L R R L L R R L L R R L *simile*
L L R R L L R R L L R R L L R

▶ Notice how one hand remains on G♯/A♭ while the other moves away from G♯/A♭ chromatically.

128

L R R L R R L R R L L R   R L L R L L R L L R L L R L L   R L L R
L L R L L R L L R L L R L   R R L R R L R R L R R L R R L   R R L R

131A ($\sqcap$ = $\sqcap^3\,\flat$)

I7

IV7

V7   IV7   I7

B ($\sqcap$ = $\sqcap^3\,\flat$)

I7

IV7   I7

V7   IV7   I7

▶ Write in the stickings that work best for you.
▶ These exercises can be played with 130. BLUES CHORD ACCOMPANIMENT on page 35.

ADVANCED FOUR MALLET STUDIES

▶ Practice exercises B and C two ways: 1. Right hand only; 2. Left hand only. Rotate your wrist to create the independent strokes. Strive for a full, even sound from stroke to stroke.

▶ Play each note with the mallet indicated.

▶ Practice exercises F and G three ways: 1. Right hand only; 2. Left hand only; 3. Left hand as written, right hand simultaneously one octave higher. Also try playing exercises B and C with both hands in octaves.

ADVANCED FOUR MALLET STUDIES

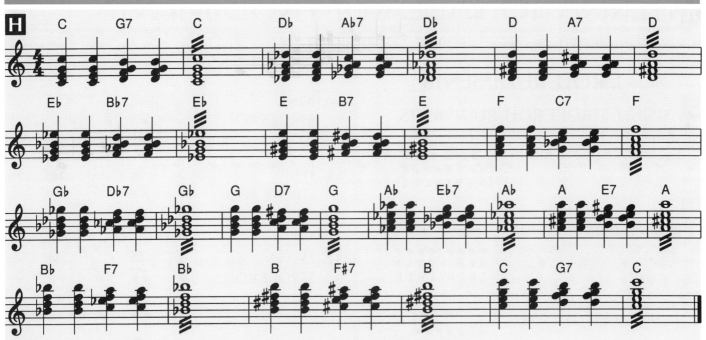

▶ The chord symbols designate the major and dominant seventh chords being played.

I Maestoso
"The Sunken Cathedral"   Claude Debussy (1862 - 1918)

ff

▶ Practice this arrangement after you learn exercise 113 on page 30. After learning to play this arrangement as written, try rolling each chord as you play.

▶ Practice this blues progression after you learn exercise 130 on page 35. This exercise can also be played with exercises 131 and 132 on page 35 and Excellerators 131A and 131B on "Mallets" page 45, cont.

▶ Play the "stems down" notes with your left hand and the "stems up" notes with your right hand.

PERCUSSIVE ARTS SOCIETY INTERNATIONAL DRUM RUDIMENTS

▶ All Rudiments should be practiced: *open* (slow) to *close* (fast) to *open* (slow) and/or at an even, moderate march tempo.

I. ROLL RUDIMENTS

A. SINGLE STROKE ROLL RUDIMENTS

1. SINGLE STROKE ROLL*

R L R L R L R L

2. SINGLE STROKE FOUR

R L R L   R L R L
L R L R   L R L R

3. SINGLE STROKE SEVEN

R L R L R L R
L R L R L R L

B. MULTIPLE BOUNCE ROLL RUDIMENTS

4. MULTIPLE BOUNCE ROLL

5. TRIPLE STROKE ROLL

R R R L L L R R R L L L

C. DOUBLE STROKE OPEN ROLL RUDIMENTS

6. DOUBLE STROKE OPEN ROLL*

R R L L R R L L

7. FIVE STROKE ROLL*

R R L L

8. SIX STROKE ROLL

R   L R   L
L   R L   R

9. SEVEN STROKE ROLL*

R   L R   L
L   R L   R

10. NINE STROKE ROLL*

R   R L   L

11. TEN STROKE ROLL*

R   R L   R   R L
L   L R   L   L R

12. ELEVEN STROKE ROLL*

R   R L   R   R L
L   L R   L   L R

13. THIRTEEN STROKE ROLL*

R   R L   L

14. FIFTEEN STROKE ROLL*

R   L R   L
L   R L   R

15. SEVENTEEN STROKE ROLL

R   R L   L

II. DIDDLE RUDIMENTS

16. SINGLE PARADIDDLE*

R L R R L R L L

17. DOUBLE PARADIDDLE*

R L R L R R L R L R L L

18. TRIPLE PARADIDDLE

R L R L R L R R L R L R L R L L

19. SINGLE PARADIDDLE-DIDDLE
R L R R L L R L R R L L
L R L L R R L R L L R R

*These Rudiments are also included in the original Standard 26 American Drum Rudiments.

Reprinted by permission of the Percussive Arts Society, Inc., P. O. Box 25, Lawton, OK 73502.

III. FLAM RUDIMENTS

20. FLAM*

21. FLAM ACCENT*

22. FLAM TAP*

23. FLAMACUE*

24. FLAM PARADIDDLE*

25. SINGLE FLAMMED MILL

26. FLAM PARADIDDLE-DIDDLE*

27. PATAFLAFLA

28. SWISS ARMY TRIPLET

29. INVERTED FLAM TAP

30. FLAM DRAG

IV. DRAG RUDIMENTS

31. DRAG*

32. SINGLE DRAG TAP*

33. DOUBLE DRAG TAP*

34. LESSON 25*

35. SINGLE DRAGADIDDLE

36. DRAG PARADIDDLE #1*

37. DRAG PARADIDDLE #2*

38. SINGLE RATAMACUE*

39. DOUBLE RATAMACUE*

40. TRIPLE RATAMACUE*

MALLET PERCUSSION INSTRUMENTS

There are many different types of mallet percussion instruments. With occassional octave transposition of the music, most of the exercises in this book can be played on any of the mallet instruments shown below.

Bells (also called a **glockenspiel** or **orchestra bells**) have metal bars and are played with hard plastic, rubber, or wood mallets.

BELLS

The **marimba** has wooden or synthetic bars and a resonating tube under each bar. It is played with soft or medium yarn or rubber mallets.

MARIMBA

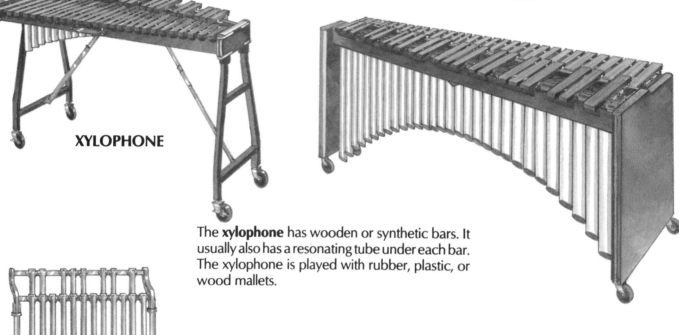

XYLOPHONE

The **xylophone** has wooden or synthetic bars. It usually also has a resonating tube under each bar. The xylophone is played with rubber, plastic, or wood mallets.

CHIMES

VIBRAPHONE

Chimes (also called **tubular bells**) are long hanging metal tubes, usually supported on a frame. Most sets of chimes also have a damper pedal, used to control ringing. Chimes are played with rawhide, wood, plastic, or hard rubber hammers.

The **vibraphone** (also called **vibes** or **vibraharp**) has metal bars and a resonating tube under each bar. It also has a damper pedal to control the ringing of the bars, and a motor-rotated disk in each resonator which can be used to create a pulsating, vibrato effect. The vibraphone is usually played with rubber or yarn mallets.

MALLET PERCUSSION
KEYBOARD LAYOUT/NOTE CHART

While each mallet instrument has its own special sound, they all have basically the same keyboard layout, like the one shown below. (Actual range of notes depends on the instrument.)

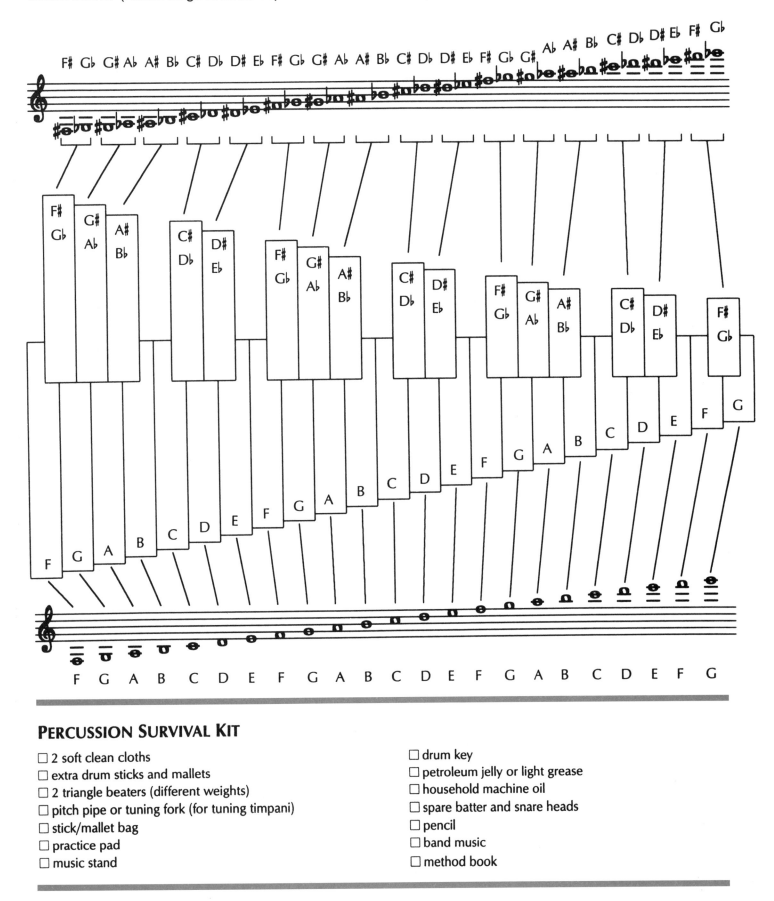

PERCUSSION SURVIVAL KIT

☐ 2 soft clean cloths
☐ extra drum sticks and mallets
☐ 2 triangle beaters (different weights)
☐ pitch pipe or tuning fork (for tuning timpani)
☐ stick/mallet bag
☐ practice pad
☐ music stand

☐ drum key
☐ petroleum jelly or light grease
☐ household machine oil
☐ spare batter and snare heads
☐ pencil
☐ band music
☐ method book

Drums

STANDARD OF EXCELLENCE

EXERCISE 9
- [ ] rhythm
- [ ] flam accents
- [ ] flams
- [ ] grip
- [ ] B.D. tech.

EXERCISE 14
- [ ] rhythm
- [ ] grip
- [ ] hand position
- [ ] posture
- [ ] stroke

EXERCISE 19
- [ ] rhythm
- [ ] rolls
- [ ] dynamics
- [ ] accents
- [ ] B.D. tech.

EXERCISE 23
- [ ] rhythm
- [ ] 5 stroke rolls
- [ ] 7 stroke rolls
- [ ] 13 stroke roll
- [ ] dynamics

EXERCISE 28
- [ ] rhythm
- [ ] 7 stroke rolls
- [ ] flams
- [ ] dynamics
- [ ] B.D. tech.

EXERCISE 32
- [ ] rhythm
- [ ] triple parads.
- [ ] flams
- [ ] dynamics
- [ ] *simile*

EXERCISE 37
- [ ] rhythm
- [ ] S. Cym. tech.
- [ ] B.D. tech.
- [ ] tone
- [ ] dynamics

EXERCISE 40
- [ ] rhythm
- [ ] 13 stroke rolls
- [ ] sticking
- [ ] tempo
- [ ] B.D. tech.

EXERCISE 41
- [ ] rhythm
- [ ] grip
- [ ] hand position
- [ ] posture
- [ ] stroke

EXERCISE 45
- [ ] rhythm
- [ ] 9 stroke rolls
- [ ] 13 stroke rolls
- [ ] 2-meas. repeat
- [ ] tempo

EXERCISE 53
- [ ] rhythm
- [ ] single ratamacues
- [ ] flamacues
- [ ] triple parads.
- [ ] repeat sign

EXERCISE 58
- [ ] rhythm
- [ ] 7 stroke rolls
- [ ] sticking
- [ ] grip
- [ ] stroke

EXERCISE 60
- [ ] rhythm
- [ ] 7 stroke rolls
- [ ] sticking
- [ ] grip
- [ ] B.D. tech.

EXERCISE 64
- [ ] rhythm
- [ ] triple ratamacues
- [ ] sticking
- [ ] grip
- [ ] stroke

EXERCISE 68
- [ ] rhythm
- [ ] trills
- [ ] time signature
- [ ] *grazioso*
- [ ] dynamics

EXERCISE 73
- [ ] rhythm
- [ ] paradiddle-diddles
- [ ] grip
- [ ] hand position
- [ ] stroke

EXERCISE 77
- [ ] rhythm
- [ ] double ratamacues
- [ ] dynamics
- [ ] tempo
- [ ] 2-meas. repeat

EXERCISE 82
- [ ] rhythm
- [ ] grace notes
- [ ] tempo
- [ ] articulation
- [ ] *dolce*

EXERCISE 86
- [ ] rhythm
- [ ] flam paradiddle-diddles
- [ ] grip
- [ ] hand position
- [ ] stroke

EXERCISE 89
- [ ] rhythm
- [ ] rolls
- [ ] flam parads.
- [ ] flam paradiddle-diddles
- [ ] B.D. tech.

EXERCISE 94
- [ ] rhythm
- [ ] drags
- [ ] sticking
- [ ] posture
- [ ] stroke

EXERCISE 98
- [ ] rhythm
- [ ] drag parads.
- [ ] grip
- [ ] hand position
- [ ] stroke

EXERCISE 102
- [ ] rhythm
- [ ] time signature
- [ ] rolls
- [ ] grace notes
- [ ] *sostenuto*

EXERCISE 106
- [ ] rhythm
- [ ] double drag taps
- [ ] grip
- [ ] hand position
- [ ] stroke

EXERCISE 108
- [ ] rhythm
- [ ] time signature
- [ ] rolls
- [ ] dynamics
- [ ] *cantabile*

EXERCISE 109
- [ ] rhythm
- [ ] coordination
- [ ] fills
- [ ] hand position
- [ ] posture

EXERCISE 117
- [ ] rhythm
- [ ] 15 stroke rolls
- [ ] drags
- [ ] dynamics
- [ ] *sfz*

EXERCISE 121
- [ ] rhythm
- [ ] 11 stroke rolls
- [ ] sticking
- [ ] grip
- [ ] stroke

EXERCISE 123
- [ ] rhythm
- [ ] time signature
- [ ] grace notes
- [ ] rolls
- [ ] *fp*

EXERCISE 132
- [ ] rhythm
- [ ] *swing*
- [ ] Brush tech.
- [ ] hand position
- [ ] coordination

EXCELLENCE

Use this chart to record your progress on the "Drums" pages.